to
GOD
from
MOM

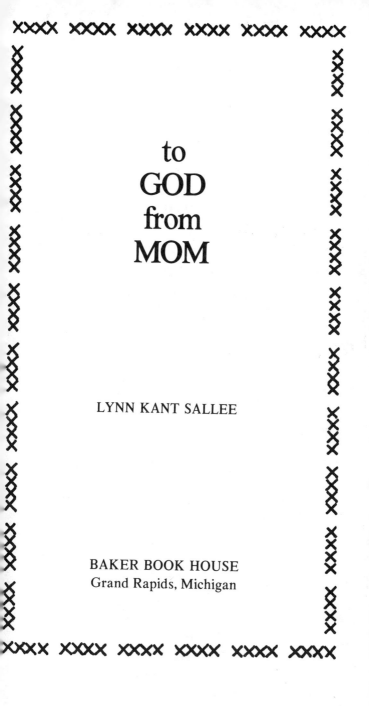

to
GOD
from
MOM

LYNN KANT SALLEE

BAKER BOOK HOUSE
Grand Rapids, Michigan

to
KELLY JEAN
and
SEAN CHRISTIAN

CONTENTS

AND SHE BROUGHT FORTH . . .

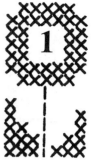

The day has finally arrived! Nine months seems so long to wait. I didn't think today would ever come. But then, just when I couldn't stand to see my swollen body reflected in the mirror one more time, labor began. God started that wondrous process of bringing forth a new human being.

I'm excited. This tiny child, grown and nourished in my body is yet a stranger to me. Is it a girl or a boy? Will it look like me, or resemble my husband? Or maybe, most likely I guess, will it be a blending of us both, a brand new individual? More important, will it be a whole and healthy baby? In just a few more minutes these questions will have answers.

But I must confess that I'm frightened, too. I know the books all say that childbirth is a natural process. They tell me that few mothers die in labor anymore, thanks to the advances in science and medicine. Still I worry. Deep down inside lurks the thought that I might become a statistic on the mortality charts.

Another contraction is beginning. My body arches, not so much in pain, but as though it were ruled by the overwhelming vitality of new life eager to see the light of the outside world. My hands rest on the great mound of pulsating activity and impatience overtakes me. Let's get on with it! I've labored long and I'm weary. Let me finish my task and sink into the welcome depths of sleep.

GOD, now that the end is near, give me strength to bear this child in dignity and with courage. Calm my rootless anxiety. Chase away the shadowy demons of fear which seem to possess me. Free me to concentrate all my energy on bringing forth a new life.

Bless, Oh, God, this child whose tiny head even now pushes downward seeking to escape from the warmth and security of my womb. No longer will I be able to protect him from every hurt. Now he will know pain, unhappiness, heartbreak, for this is the price we all must pay for the joy of being. I pray that You'll send him the sustaining gift of faith to support him as he stumbles down the paths of life.

I need Your blessings, too, God. I confess that I'm not worthy of the great trust You've placed in me. I'm lacking in many of the virtues a good mother needs: wisdom, compassion, patience, warmth. I face the awesome responsibility of motherhood relying on Your love to give me direction. Help me to guide and shape this child so he will grow in Your image and follow in Your footsteps.

from MOM (Almost!)

2 A.M. AND ALL IS WELL!

I'm so tired. It seemed like I'd just closed my eyes when I heard that lusty wail telling me my baby was hungry again. How I hate to leave the soft comforting warmth of my bed. I've had a tiring day—washing diapers, preparing bottles, bathing, changing, feeding, all those necessary but time-consuming duties of a new mother. Couldn't I pretend I don't hear? Maybe it's not time yet. Maybe he'll fall back to sleep if I lay here quietly a few minutes.

But no, the protests only grow more vigorous, more frequent. My husband tosses restlessly, his sleep disturbed by the crying. The luminous dial on the clock glares out the truth I've evaded—it's 2 o'clock, time to rise and feed my baby.

LORD, give me strength to accept this responsibility of motherhood, much as I resent the intrusion on my rest. Guide my slippered feet to the kitchen. Keep me awake during that seemingly endless wait for the bottle to warm. Let my touch be gentle, my smile warm as I cradle my infant in my arms to feed him. And then, Lord, when his tummy is full and the burp has finally come up, let us both fall back to sleep quickly and rest peacefully 'til morning.

from MOM

A GIANT STEP
FOR MANKIND

I didn't think he'd ever let go of the edge of the coffee table to try a step alone. Week after week he worked his way carefully from table to couch to wall and back again. His chubby legs seemed just a trifle unsteady and he tested the floor with his toe each time before he'd commit himself to putting his foot down, but still he seemed strong and ready to walk.

How many times did I watch him as he looked wishfully across an empty space and considered trying to cover the distance in an upright position, only to decide at the last minute not to chance it? He'd plop down on hands and knees and creep to his destination, a more familiar and trusted form of locomotion. I'd release the breath I'd been holding and hope . . . maybe next time.

But today the urge to try overcame his inhibitions. He pushed himself away from the table and stood there, swaying back and forth for a moment. Then, one step, another, and plop down on his behind. That first step seemed every bit as important to me as the astronauts' first walk on the moon. Both were truly giant steps for mankind!

GOD, I thank You for giving me a strong, healthy child. His first step was awkward and unsteady. I wanted to rush to him, to walk beside him, to shelter and protect him from the pain of a fall. Soon he'll be more confident and, later, when he's able to run and skip and hop, he won't remember how difficult was the challenge of his first step. But even as he grows in ability, won't You walk beside him? Please be there to shelter and protect him from a fall far more serious than any he might have taken today, a fall from Your grace and love.

from MOM

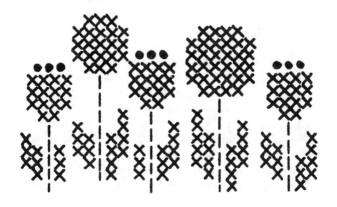

4

WET AGAIN!

LORD, I'm so upset and frustrated that I don't know if I can express myself coherently. Not even to You who I approach today with a prayer for greater patience and a plea for more strength. Two weeks, that's fourteen whole days, Lord, I've worked on potty training my child.

I sit with him by the hour (at least it seems that long), perched on the edge of the tub, encouraging him to put something in the plastic container attached to his potty chair. My mind is worn out with thinking of new ways to entertain him so he'll stay put on that tiny wooden seat. He's truly king for the day, sitting there on his throne watching the court jester put on a performance.

Then there's the soaring water consumption. My husband will go through the ceiling when he sees this month's utility bill! I try to run just a slow trickle to inspire him. The baby manuals all assured me that the trick never fails—only it did. Gallons and gallons of water gurgled down the drain but not a drop of urine fell into the potty!

I've tried coaxing and pleading, kissing and hugging, and even, in desperation, out-and-out bribery with pennies and lollipops. He licks the lollipops down to the stick, makes a few token grunts, and then hops off the seat only to reappear a few minutes later with soiled training pants or urine running down his chubby legs. Then I get angry and shout and he gets hurt and cries. It's a vicious circle of frustration and failure that's tearing us apart.

I need help, Lord. Patience, yes. Gentleness, yes. But even more than these I need perspective. In my more rational moments I realize he's not likely to enter kindergarten in diapers. I know those development charts in the baby manuals are only a guide, not a decree that every child will be potty trained by such-and-such a month. I'm even aware of how much my desire to see him trained hinges upon my own need for approval from grandparents and admiration and envy of my friends and neighbors. But this logical reasoning gets distorted in the day-to-day bouts with the potty chair. The goal of training him gets blown up out of proportion until it seems of paramount importance.

So I pray today that You'll give me a proper perspective for tomorrow. Help me accept the failures and still retain a hope for success the next time. Give me the strength to look at his soggy training pants and say "Better luck next time" instead of shouting "Wet again!"

from MOM

5

TEMPERATURE 102, AND RISING

Two watery eyes sunk back in my child's face were my first warning of trouble to come. Then his nose began to flow in an annoyingly steady stream. A wastebasket filled with used tissues explains the tender redness around his nostrils. The cough came next, a steady hack that seemed to tear from the bottom of his stomach, shaking his body. When his temperature began to push the line on the thermometer past 98.6, I wasn't really surprised. Yet another symptom of the "common" cold.

I've never understood why it's called the *common* cold. The multitude of symptoms and acute discomfort it brings with it seem very uncommon to me. My miserable child can't sleep because the cough keeps him awake. Yet he's tired from the physically draining effects of fever. He's lost his appetite. Not even his favorite foods can tempt him when his throat is raw. A strong odor of Vicks pervades his bedroom and a vaporizer hums and hisses, belching forth steam to help him breathe easier. One sick child plus one concerned and harried mother add up to a totally disrupted household. I just wish he'd hurry up and get well so things can settle back to a normal routine!

GOD, sometimes I take my child's excellent health for granted. I forget that the worst sickness he's known is an occasional cold or stomach flu or ear infection. Leukemia, muscular dystrophy, sickle-cell anemia, and cancer are just words to him, vague diseases he hears about on television but which don't affect him personally. Let me take this opportunity to thank You that he's never known the torture of prolonged pain, the frustration of physical or mental efforts, the hopelessness and despair of a terminal illness. I pray that he never will.

Thank You, too, for the medical advances which make my child's sickness far less serious than it would have been in my grandmother's day. Antibiotics and aspirin, decongestants and cough medicines, all help him feel more comfortable and recover more quickly. Perhaps only the mother of a sick child can really appreciate these gifts of healing.

If I don't find much time to talk with You these next few days (I know I've been neglecting You all week), please understand, Father. A sick child requires a lot of attention and much care. He wants an opponent to play checkers, a companion to watch cartoons, an admirer for his colored pictures. There are pills to give, a chest to rub, the vaporizer to fill, malts to make, and a hundred other little needs I must meet. But isn't this the purpose for which You created mothers? To love and care for their families?

from MOM

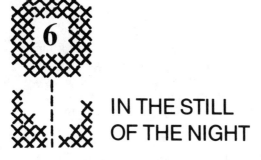

IN THE STILL
OF THE NIGHT

Somewhere from the depths of sleep a child's cries reach me and drag me, unwilling and fighting, back to wakefulness. The bedroom is dark. My husband sleeps on undisturbed, not blessed with that special mother's instinct which flashes a red light of warning when her child wakes. The whimpers push aside the stillness of the night.

What's the matter this time? Another imaginary grizzly bear threatening from the closet? (I bravely shooed an elephant out of his room just two nights ago!) Perhaps a crack of lightning zig-zagging across the sky? Maybe just a nightmare formed in an over-active mind that won't settle down peacefully to rest? Who but a mother knows the countless reasons children wake at night?

Sometimes I get so impatient with this night duty. Especially on a night like tonight which follows a busy day. I'm bone tired. My every selfish instinct tells me to stay in bed. The thunderstorm will pass, the nightmare will fade, eventually even the grizzly bear will dissolve in the reality of the sunrise. I'd like to bury my head under the pillow and pretend not to hear, only it wouldn't work. I'd still *know* even if I couldn't hear. I must get out of bed and calm my wakeful child.

He's asleep now, *GOD*. It didn't take long. He wasn't sick; and for that I thank You. It was only a nightmare but it seemed very real to him. He needed the few light strokes across his forehead, the softly whispered words of comfort and understanding, the gentle tucking in of blankets around his tearstained face. Then his eyelids drooped and he fell asleep with a smile on his face.

In these wee hours of the morning, I realized the beautiful, yet awesome, power of a mother's love. My child has faith in me. He truly believes I can chase away elephants and grizzly bears single-handed. He looks to me for protection and comfort when he's worried or frightened. When I think of that great trust he has in me, I'm ashamed for my earlier selfish thoughts. I gave up five or ten minutes of sleep so that he could rest peacefully. That wasn't much of a sacrifice, was it? No tremendous effort on my part, yet the rewards of looking down on my child's face as he sleeps are great. Help me to remember this rare moment of insight the next time he wakes in the night and calls out, *Mommy!*

from MOM

7

I WANNA' BE FREE!

Whatever happened to the little boy who wanted mommy to do everything for him? The one who depended on me to squeeze toothpaste on his brush, lay out his play clothes, and cut his meat into bite-sized pieces? He surely doesn't live in my home anymore!

This strange child who's come to live with me has a mind of his own. "Let me do it." "I can do that all by myself." "I don't want any help." A totally independent creature is he. He can pour his milk and wash his hands without assistance. He *thinks* he can make his own bed and handle spaghetti without having it cut into shorter strands. Could this self-sufficient child and the dependent boy who used to live here be one and the same?

GOD, I'm not sure that I like this child as well as the old version. It's nice to feel needed, to have someone depend on you. But I guess I'd better start adjusting to his independent ways because he will continue to grow, to develop new capabilities, and to assume more and greater responsibilities. In my heart, I know I wouldn't want him to stay a baby all his life. But somewhere, in some small hidden corner, a voice reminds me that he's moving away from me. He's holding me away from him and crying out, "I wanna' be free!"

Please, Father, help me loosen up the apron strings a little. Give me the courage to let him try. Sometimes he will make mistakes, errors in judgment due to immaturity. He will know defeat and frustration, pain and sadness. But I can't walk with him through life, always ready to shield and protect. Like a mother bird, I must push him out of the nest and let him try his wings.

But when independence gets to be too much for him, when he wants to take time off to be a little boy again, I'll rock him on my lap and smile, thinking back to the past and looking ahead to what the future holds for him.

from MOM

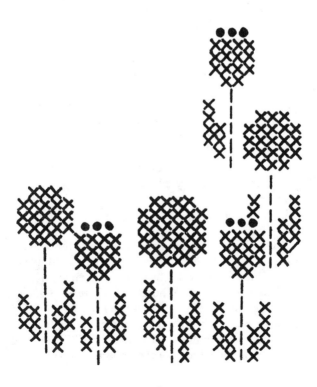

ALONE AT LAST

Day after day, week after week, the constant responsibility for children gets to be quite a weight on this mother's shoulders. How often I've wished they could go away and leave me alone for a little while. Now they have. I'm alone at last!

Grandma willingly accepted, even requested, my responsibility for a week. The children seemed as eager to go as she was to have them and I was to have them go. Perhaps day after day with mother isn't all that thrilling either.

The first day of solitude seemed like heaven. I visited three antique shops, took a long bubble bath in the middle of the afternoon, sewed up a dress in one sitting without once getting up to apply a band aid, and fixed a candlelight dinner for just the two of us.

But already that exciting newness has begun to fade. The house seems awfully quiet after my husband leaves for work. I turn on the radio for company, some noise to fill the empty silence. After lunch, I called grandma's, long distance, to talk with the children. I miss those little stinkers!

GOD, help me to use this opportunity for solitude to grow. It's a chance to refresh myself mentally, physically, and spiritually. In the quiet of an empty house I have time to question. Who am I? Where am I going? What are my goals in life? How can I reach them? Too often these questions get buried under the laundry and dirty dishes. Now that I have time for self-study and self-evaluation, let me use the opportunity wisely and grow in greater knowledge of myself and my faith in You.

I'm reminded, Lord, that soon the children will grow up and leave home. The years pass by so swiftly and I haven't prepared for that stage of my life. The house will seem empty then, too. The quiet will oppress and depress me as it does now. Help me ready myself for a deserted nest. Teach me to build friendships, develop interests and talents, grow as a person, so I'll have something to fill the void when the children leave permanently.

Finally, Father, thank you for blessing me with a family to love and care for. I appreciate these children so much more when they're absent than when they're present. From the bottom of a mother's heart I pray that You'll make your face to shine upon them all the days of their lives.

from MOM

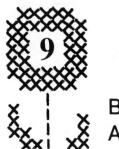

BUTTONS
AND BOWS

I never realized before today how complex and complicated the process of tying a bow really is. Perhaps back in the netherworld of my mind memories of my own first clumsy attempts are stored, but I can't recall them. Years of practice have taught me to perform the task effortlessly, almost without thinking. That certainly isn't true of my child!

I spent the better part of the day instructing my four-year-old in the art of tying a bow. Heads bent over an old tennis shoe, we labored together. "Let me show you once more," I'd say. He'd watch closely, then announce, "I'll try it now." Awkward little fingers would manipulate the floppy lace, pushing, pulling, forming giant loops—all in vain.

"Just once more," I'd urged, "and then we'll call it quits for today." Lo and behold, he tied a bow! Not perfect, of course. One loop was much longer than the other, the knot wasn't very tight, and the plastic tip of one end extended a mere half inch from the knot—but a beautiful bow nonetheless. His face shone forth pride in achievement. He'd reached toward a goal, failed many times, but finally succeeded.

FATHER, I'm grateful for the opportunity to watch my child learn and to help him along the way. Today I was witness to the almost magical process of growing up. New skills, developing talents, growing mind and body are all a part of my child's daily life. Each morning he wakes a different child than the day before—somehow altered by the experiences of yesterdays.

I'm thankful, too, Lord, that You gave me patience to supervise his many attempts without losing my temper. So many times I wanted to blurt out, "It's so easy. Why can't you do it?" But You helped me hold back the cruel words which would only have hurt his feelings and cut off any further efforts. Now I pray that You'll give me more patience to untie all the bows and knots he made this evening as he practiced his new-found skill—on the drapery cords, my apron strings, daddy's robe belt, and sister's jump rope!

from MOM

WHERE DID I COME FROM?

Standing in line at the checkout counter wasn't my choice of an ideal location for beginning my child's sex education, but it suited him just fine. After several minutes spent in fascinated study of the very pregnant woman behind us, my child asked in a voice which could be heard all the way back to the meat counter, "Does that lady have a baby in her tummy?"

My face must have made ten color changes from pink all the way to crimson before I mumbled an affirmative answer. I hoped that would end the discussion. But, no, the questions came flowing out like soda out of an overturned pop can.

"Isn't the baby all scrunched up in there? Doesn't it hurt when he kicks her in the stomach? When will it come out? How does it get born?" And then the clincher: "How did it get in there?"

I struggled to answer his questions, mostly in monosyllables, while the store manager, two clerks, the checkout girl, and an assortment of customers listened in amusement to my stuttering. Longer explanations, I felt, could wait until we and our groceries were safely in the car.

I'm sorry I bungled the job so badly. My surprise and lack of preparation and embarrassment made this introduction to the wonders of sex far from satisfactory. I wanted to present sex information to my child in a natural, relaxed manner. But somehow I'd expected the questions to come at night when I was tucking him into bed. I never planned on hearing them in the grocery store!

FATHER, You made man and woman in Your own image. The beauty of the human body, the tremendous power of love and the satisfactions of expressing that deep feeling for another human being in the closeness of physical union are not subjects to be dismissed in a single mumbled word. They are natural and beautiful expressions of our humanity.

Please help me, Lord, to convey the wonders of sex to my child. Guide me in the future when he comes to me with questions so I can speak from my heart and soul without hesitation or uneasiness. Help me unfold the mysteries of love and sex, maleness and femaleness, gradually as he matures and searches for answers to his questions.

Remind my husband, and me too, Lord, that our marriage is a living example for our child. Help us to build our lives together in love and Christian faith so he will have a good model to follow in his own life.

from MOM

SURPRISE, MOMMY!

While I was busy scrubbing the bathroom floor my child was busy at the kitchen counter—peeling apples. I'd started working on the rosy pile earlier but two pies later I'd decided I was due for a break. Leaving the peeler and a bowl half full of apple slices, I'd taken bucket in hand and trudged upstairs to tackle the only job I hate worse than peeling apples.

You wouldn't believe the mess one child and a pile of apples can make! Peels covered the floor, seeds stuck to the wallpaper, juice ran in streaks to his elbows. I was about to scold when I looked into the bowl—it was nearly full, and several more apples, shorn of their skins, needed only to be sliced. True, the slices were irregular and a trifle thick. A few bits of red still clung to the white flesh and some bruises remained, but the job was nearly done. "I help mommy," my child said proudly, and I thanked him with my biggest hug.

GOD, it's rewarding to watch my child grow in ability and to see him exhibit such thoughtfulness for others. He knew how much I hated to peel apples so he offered his assistance. Perhaps it seems like just a little act of kindness to You but it meant a whole lot to me.

Wouldn't the world be a much better place if we all learned, like my small child, to offer our help to each other?

from MOM

THE TOOTH FAIRY FLIES AGAIN!

I'd begun to think that baby tooth would never give up its grasp on my child's gums! We wiggled it, jiggled it, even tried sticky caramel apples and wads of bubble gum. Still it hung on stubbornly to a slender strand of skin. Finally, in desperation, we turned to the old string-on-the-doorknob trick and out it popped.

Now that tiny white pearl rests under the pillow and my child dreams happily that the tooth fairy flies again. Visions of a winged sylph jingling with nickels, dimes, and quarters will provide entertainment through the night.

GOD, thinking of that tooth lying under the pillow, I thank You for the abundant food You provided to nourish it. Strong and healthy, free from decay, it is truly a reflection of the good life You've given us. My child has never known the terrible gnawing of hunger which causes weak and deformed bodies. For this I'm grateful, God.

Thank You, too, for providing the shiny quarter which will delight my child tomorrow morning. An empty-handed tooth fairy would be a crushing disillusionment.

Finally, I ask Your assistance in my magical mission tonight. Give my hands a fairy-light touch as I fumble under the pillow for that tiny tooth and replace it with the quarter. Let my child sleep on, undisturbed, smiling in anticipation of tomorrow.

from MOM

I MADE IT
MYSELF

For days my child has mysteriously confined himself to the garage from the minute he steps off the school bus until I call him in for dinner. Questions about his activities bring a cryptic mumbled answer, "Working." When I approach the vicinity of the garage he blocks the door with his small body, arms stretched wide from jamb to jamb, and tells me to go away or I'll ruin the surprise.

Just before dinner tonight he came into the kitchen where I was working. His appearance was a mother's nightmare! Green paint streaked down the front of his shirt and school pants. Daubs of emerald spotted his face, neck, even his hair.

I opened my mouth to scold but before I could get the words out, he revealed something he'd been hiding behind his back. "Surprise, Mom, I made it myself." I stared at the object, puzzled. "It's a bird house," he explained, his face crumpling and the brightness dying out of his eyes. "Don't you like it?"

GOD, you must have been listening because you provided just the right words of praise to bring the smile back to my child's lips. And it was a beautiful bird house, wasn't it? Constructed of popsicle sticks and painted bright green because he knows it's my favorite color, it was one of the finest gifts I've ever received. It was a gift of love, a gift he created with the labor of his own hands in the true spirit of giving.

Thank You, Father, for this loving, sharing, giving child—and for a very special bird house already hanging from a branch of the apple tree in our backyard.

from MOM

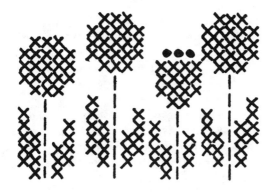

14

ON
ROLLER SKATES
AND
BICYCLES

This afternoon I took a break from my housework to sit at the window and watch the neighborhood children playing. My son, just learning to ride a bicycle, worked diligently to acquire this new skill. The bicycle wobbled down the driveway, swerving to miss the lilac bush, as uncertain hands turned the handlebars too sharply and sent the vehicle off course. Then he was flying through the air, a whirling mass of limbs.

Staring at his crumpled body lying on the lawn, I was halfway out of my chair to go to him when he slowly sat up. Carefully he examined knees and elbows, then shook himself loose, and climbed back on his bicycle. Did I imagine it, or was the bike a little steadier when he rode past me again, waving when he saw me at the window?

Across the street a young girl tried out her new roller skates. Like my child, she lost her balance and fell, skinning her knee on the sidewalk. Home she ran, and into the house. But to my surprise, she reappeared a few minutes later sporting a band aid on her injured knee. She put those skates back on and tried once more.

I learned something today, *GOD*, as I watched those children play. They have a special kind of courage: the courage to fall, to hurt, but to get back up and try again. A skinned knee, a bumped head, doesn't stop them for long.

Maybe once I, too, possessed that courage, that determination to succeed. No longer. Each time I fall, each time I fail, I find it a little harder to get up and try again. I throw up my hands and say "What's the use?" I lay back and moan, nursing my hurts, afraid to face being hurt again.

Help me, God, to recapture that resilience I knew in my youth. Give me back the courage to try, to fail, and to try again. Otherwise the talents, the skills, the intelligence You gave me will never be fully developed. I will always be less of a person than You have a right to expect.

Now that I finally realize the value of patience and persistence, help me to pass this new-found knowledge on to my children. Show me how to comfort them in their pains of defeat—but also to encourage them to keep on trying.

When faith doesn't come easily, give them the grace to keep searching. When they listen but You are silent, give them patience to wait until You're ready to communicate. If You've given them any special gifts— musical, artistic, literary, or scientific talents—give them also the persistence to develop Your gift to the fullest and to use it for Your greater glory.

Help these children (and their mother) get back on the bicycle or the roller skates just one more time!

from MOM

DEAR MOMMY AND DADDY

The postman brought a special envelope in this morning's mail. It was addressed in a wobbly elementary school penmanship and, inside, a many-folded sheet of stationery began "Dear Mommy and Daddy". I chuckled aloud at the lines of pencil writing running uphill across the page. But then, when I got to the end a tear sneaked out of my eye and rolled down my cheek. "Very truly your," the closing read. So formal, so correct—straight from a fourth grade unit on letter writing. It clashed with the row of X's following the PS. My child's first letter home will, I'm sure, become a precious and treasured souvenir of his childhood as the years pass.

LORD, I'm reminded today how vitally important open lines of communication are to any relationship. Right now my child is willing, even eager, to share his thoughts and dreams, disappointments and failures with me. But I fear that as he grows older that openness will disappear. So many of us, with maturity, lose the ability to communicate with those we love, even with You. Letters we intend to write never get written, phone calls we intend to make never get dialed, words we intend to say never get spoken.

I pray that my child will always have someone he can communicate with. If he can't come to me or his father, I hope he'll find his way to You. It's reassuring to know that You'll be listening.

from MOM

I TOUCHED THEM

16

I forget now what their argument was about. Perhaps a toy they both wanted to play with. Maybe the last cookie in the jar. The point is, I'd had enough of their squabbling. "Cut it out!" I yelled. "Can't you two ever get along?"

Their faces crinkled up and tears began to roll. Impulsively, I threw an arm around each of them and hugged them tightly. They snuggled up against me and each other. Fights and tears were forgotten for the moment as we communicated with each other by touch.

GOD, I often forget the power of a hug or a friendly tousling of hair, or a hand to hold. When my children were infants we had to communicate mainly by touch because they couldn't speak. I held them, rocked them, played with tiny fingers and toes. But as they learned to talk I gradually eliminated touching and substituted words for caresses.

Help me to remember that none of us ever outgrows our need for that unique and special closeness of communication by touch. Let me reach out to my children more often. Remind me that I have to show them I love them, not just tell them. Sometimes words alone are not enough. Yes, sometimes a single touch speaks more loudly, more clearly, than a string of eloquent syllables.

from MOM

NO TIME
FOR
PAPER DOLLS

All day long the children pestered me to play with them. They wanted stories read, a snowman built, and help with a jigsaw puzzle. But most of all, my daughter wanted help with her new paper dolls. Unfortunately, they weren't the punch-out type. All those tiny clothes with their hundreds of tabs had to be cut out with a scissors, a task much too difficult for her.

When she asked in the morning I was sorting laundry. "Later," I told her. But the day flew by as I rushed from one task to another and I never did make time for paper dolls or puzzles or snowmen.

As I shaped the meatloaf for dinner, I overheard my daughter talking to her dolls. "I don't have time to play right now. Can't you see how busy I am? Look at me iron daddy's shirts. Now I'm going to scrub the bathroom floor. No, no time for paper dolls today." She was mimicking me!

Please, *GOD*, let me learn from that overheard conversation between a little girl and her doll. Once again I'd gotten my priorities confused. I put the laundry and dirty dishes ahead of my children's needs. Couldn't I have left the garbage cans unwashed and used that fifteen minutes to read a storybook to the children? Couldn't I have omitted the homemade apple pie from the dinner menu and cut out some paper doll clothes instead? You gave me just twenty-four hours today. It was my decision how to spend them and, looking back, I see that my choice wasn't a wise one.

The time I might have spent playing with my children today is gone. Irretrievably. The closeness we might have shared, the bonds between us we might have strengthened have been sacrificed. I cannot turn back the clock and start over again at breakfast, but I can learn from the experience. I can do a better job of mothering tomorrow.

Lord, please nudge me when I get so involved in housework and my own activities that I cheat my children out of their rightful share of mother's attention. Just whisper in my ear, "No time for paper dolls." I'll understand.

from MOM

BAKING BREAD TOGETHER

Flour dusts across her hair and streaks along one cheek. Small plump fingers, now turned white, have punched and prodded the lump of dough in joyful abandon. Now the ball of dough rests under a cloth while we wait for it to rise.

She lifts the corner of the towel again to sneak a tiny peek. Wasn't it just two minutes ago that she last looked? I can read on her face all the doubts harbored in her mind. How, she wonders, will that pasty lump become a loaf of bread?

FATHER, Your Son Jesus loved the little children. He didn't disappoint or disillusion them. For His sake, please let this bread rise high and light. It needn't be a gourmet's prize—but please, please let it rise!

* * *

Slowly it begins to swell, to double in size. "Now punch it down," I tell her. The doubts come flooding back. She doesn't believe the miracle can work twice. But it did and soon the warm and homey smell of baking bread floats through the house.

Thank You, *LORD*, for these two golden loaves—a testimony of faith created by four hands.

Today I realized, Lord, how similar my family is to that bread dough. Only a pasty mass, we really serve no purpose unless You are with us. Your grace is what causes us to swell and become something new and better just as the yeast transformed that dough into bread. Thank You, Father, for being the yeast of our lives.

from MOM

SCHOOL DAYS, SCHOOL DAYS

It feels so much like summer that I can hardly believe the calendar says September. It doesn't seem possible that all the weeks from Memorial Day to Labor Day could have flown by so fast. But I look at these children lined up by the door, dressed in crisp new clothes and stiff, shiny shoes (so soon the knees will sport patches covering the gaping holes and the shoes will be run-down and scuffed!) and I know that the first day of school has arrived. The visible proof stands right before my eyes, these scrubbed-faced children so eager and excited to return to their classrooms, friends, and teachers.

GOD, please guide the teachers who will supervise my children's learning this year. Give them patience to handle all the questions and problems that arise during the long school day. Give them tolerance and understanding, too. Expecially if my kindergartener wets her pants occasionally and my older child still hasn't mastered the multiplication tables. I'm grateful for the fine, dedicated teachers in our school system. Bless them and their efforts, Father.

My children will need Your guidance, too. Open their minds so they can absorb the knowledge their books and teachers will provide. Help them discover the pure joy of learning for learning's sake and the satisfaction which comes from putting forth their best efforts. Armed with these tools for learning—crayons, scissors, glue, paper and pencils—they are setting out on a great journey down the road to wisdom this bright September morning.

Please, Father, watch over them and bless them as they progress along the route.

from MOM

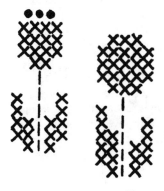

THANK YOU
FOR FATHERS

I know my husband was tired when he got home from work tonight. He'd had to put in overtime again. He was probably hungry, too. A hasty lunch snatched in a free minute was quite likely all he'd eaten since he left home early this morning. And now dinner was delayed two hours from the usual time. I watched him coming up the sidewalk. His shoulders slouched wearily.

Then the children rushed past me and burst out the door toward Daddy. The sight of them running to meet him transformed him into a new man. I could see the sunshine-warm smile lighting his lips, and its brightness reflected in his eyes. He swung each child high into the air and was rewarded with squeals of joyous delight. A tiny hand snuggled into each of his for the brief walk to the front door.

Thank you, *GOD*, for this strong yet gentle man who is my husband and the father of my children. In Your wisdom, You made parents in pairs, both a mother and a father. The job of raising a family is tremendously difficult, yet equally rewarding. Together we can share the joys and the disappointments, the sunny days and the cloudy hours. In sharing, our responsibilities are halved but our happiness is doubled. Bless our sometimes feeble attempts to rear our children in Your ways. But, even more tonight, I ask Your fullest blessings on this important person in their lives—their daddy.

from MOM

WATCH FOR MILKWEED PODS

This evening my husband had to attend a meeting and I was left alone with the children. We were clearing the dinner table when I glanced out the window and noticed what a beautiful fall evening we'd been blessed with. "Let's leave the dishes for later and go for a walk in the woods," I suggested, thinking it was a good way to pass an hour before their bedtime.

We soon set off, the kids squealing in delight and tugging my hand to pull me over to see a caterpillar, a purple thistle, some rabbit tracks cast in clay. I wasn't terribly enthusiastic at first, but slowly Nature, dressed in her vivid wardrobe of orange, red, and yellow, began to charm me. In the quiet and solitude of leaf-strewn paths, I found an inner peace and serenity I'd not known for many months.

Then the woods opened into a glen and we romped joyfully through the knee-high grasses. I spied a milk-weed pod already bursting its seams to release the precious seeds inside. Recalling a long-forgotten experience from my childhood, I called my children to me and showed them how to scatter the feathery seed parachutes, holding them high so the breeze caught them and carried them to new homes. Soon the air was filled with a white shower of fluffy milkweed seeds.

One hour passed, then another. It was dusk before we emerged from the woods, our arms laden with such treasures as empty milkweed pods, pretty brown weeds, and brightly-colored leaves. The orange harvest moon seemed to be smiling at us as we trudged along the road toward home—and I smiled back.

GOD, I'd forgotten what a gorgeous world You created for our pleasure. The joys of nature, uncrowded and unspoiled, are there for us to find every day if we seek them. Tonight I learned again to appreciate the beauty of Your handiwork.

I've learned, too, how little it takes to fill a child with happiness. A milkweed pod or a furry caterpillar is as much a source of delight as any department store toy. Help my children keep this love of simple pleasures alive into adulthood. Remind them (and their mother) to step out of the materialism of everyday life occasionally and seek the priceless gems in Nature's treasure chest.

Thank You, God, for the beauties of nature and for these children to share it with me.

from MOM

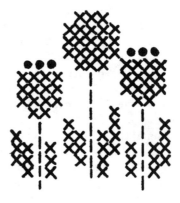

A CHILD DIED

I saw another mother's child die today. One moment she was laughing with friends as they rode their bicycles home from school; the next she swerved into the path of an oncoming car and lay dead on the hard pavement. I saw the fling of a gay plaid smock in the air, a reading book thrown from her bike basket landed near my feet on the sidewalk, long dark hair spread like a halo about her head. Yes, these things I saw and remembered but I've already blocked out the hideous memory of that jarring impact of metal on flesh and the tiny broken body of a little girl who will laugh no more. Perhaps the nightmare will return to haunt me in sleep tonight but right now, mercifully, I can put it out of my mind. What I can't forget is the chilling reminder of our mortality and the awesome finality of death.

LORD, I grieve for the mother of that little girl. My heart goes out to her as only another mother's can. Her loss must be immeasurable, her pain intolerable. Please give her strength to accept the death of her daughter and to go on with life.

I confess that I cannot understand Your purpose in taking this child's, or any child's, life. So young, so loving—children are needed as examples for all of us who call ourselves adults. "Be as a little child," You told us. I accept this child's death as Your will, but I find the acceptance extremely difficult. It reminds me that my own children are vulnerable. They, too, might be snatched away in the unyielding arms of death.

I'm selfish, Father, but I thank You that it was not my child who died today. Mine are well and safe here in their home tonight. And if they were puzzled when I hugged them so tightly as I tucked them into bed, at least You knew why.

from MOM

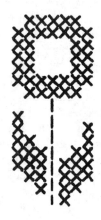

MUD PUDDLES ARE FOR WALKING THROUGH

Here they come, home from school. My children's raincoats shine like small yellow suns against the gray sky. I stand at the window and watch them near the house. Only three more mud puddles along the route to the front door—three more temptations too strong and enticing to resist. Splash, slurp, gurgle. I can almost hear the water pouring over boot tops and sloshing around on the inside. Telltale dark areas on pant legs bear testimony to the countless other puddles they've encountered and explored along the way.

Quickly, *GOD,* before they arrive, help me remember my own days of puddle stomping; those days of childhood when I wasn't concerned about wet dirty clothes because I didn't have to launder them. Help me to recapture those moments of pure ecstasy I spent ankle deep in pools of rain water. Caught up in those memories, maybe I can greet my children with a smile. Perhaps I can even strip them of wet clothes without scolding and shoo them into the kitchen for cocoa and cookies. They're kind of cute out there in the rain, aren't they? Doesn't their puddle wading make You chuckle just a little, too, Lord?

from MOM

500 MILES,
500 MILES

Maps, banana skins, and used Kleenex clutter the floor of the car, despite the two litter bags placed at strategic locations—one within arm's reach of each child. Our car, so spotlessly clean and neatly packed when we left home just a short while ago, now looks like a sanitary landfill site. I'd like to call in a bull-dozer to push a foot of dirt over the whole mess. I hesitate only because I'd have to sacrifice the three pairs of dirty socks, one sandal (we lost its mate somewhere along the interstate) and four wet swim suits which have found homes among the disposable rubbish!

What a vacation! We'd gathered around the kitchen table so many evenings planning this trip—pouring over maps, picking attractions and stops along the route, preparing a packing list so that this vacation we'd remember all the essentials we forgot last year. But something's gone wrong.

The kids have tired of "car games" and turned to other entertainment—wrestling. And one keeps insisting he's going to be car sick. They're impatient and anxious to reach our destination. I can understand their restlessness but I can't tolerate their crankiness. I don't want to listen to any more whining or griping. I don't care to hear another rendition of "How far do we have to go yet?" and the groan which invariably follows my answer. Nor do I want to show the distance graphically to my youngest child with a "We are here ... (a finger jabbed at X on the map) and we're going here" (another finger about six inches away). My finger seems to creep so slowly across the map's surface because he has to be shown every fifteen minutes.

My husband complains that his neck hurts, then his head aches, then his foot is sleeping. But when I offer to take the wheel for awhile, his pains disappear in a miraculous recovery that lasts about ten miles. I'm a bit short-tempered myself. I'd fallen asleep earlier and my husband drove right past the famous Old Clock Museum, my contribution to the agenda of scheduled stops. He says he didn't notice it!

GOD, it hurts me to see my family so torn apart. We can live in reasonable harmony at home but we can't seem to tolerate the confinement of a car or motel room. The space is too small for us to go our separate ways. We can't find the privacy we need with just a front seat and back seat or bedroom and bathroom to choose from. It's our very closeness which drives us apart.

We're all tired, too, Lord. Please give us enough sense to stop and rest. We need refreshment and a change of scenery and a chance to stretch protesting muscles. Perhaps most of all, we need to go apart from each other and seek communion with You.

Why, I wonder, does our vacation mirror our normal daily life? Why do we rush, pressured by speedometer and watch, past interesting places we'd really like to see? What's our big hurry? I wish I knew the answers.

from MOM

DADDY'S GONE A-HUNTING

The clanging alarm clock woke me well before dawn. At first I thought I'd made a mistake setting it but then, from down the hall, I heard the echo of my sons's feet hitting the floor. My husband groaned only once before pulling himself into a sitting position on the edge of the bed. Only one thing could possibly account for their prompt early rising—opening day of hunting season.

I fed them mountains of pancakes and sausage patties, packed a lunch which could keep a small regiment on its feet for a week, and pushed them out the door. Chattering happily, the camouflage-clad pair hurried off into the darkness. My son's first hunting expedition.

GOD, as I sit here at the kitchen table over a cup of coffee, scanning the horizon for some hint of the rising sun, I can't help worrying. My son looked so young dressed in those baggy, hand-me-down hunting clothes. Does he have the experience and maturity to hunt safely? I pray he does, but I still worry. I guess I'll feel uneasy until I see their safe return this evening. Please watch over them today and protect them from harm, these two important men in my life. And if, in Your wisdom, You see fit to send a duck flying low over my son's head, this mother will be very grateful.

from MOM

OBITUARY FOR RAGGEDY ANN

26

"I think I'll sell my dolls at your rummage sale, Mom," she said at the breakfast table this morning.

"Which ones, darling?" I asked as I flipped another pancake from pan to plate.

"All of them. I'm getting too old to play with dolls."

I should have seen her growing. I should have noticed that she doesn't play with her dolls anymore. She doesn't spend hours dressing them, bathing them, feeding them, even talking to them like she used to do. The baby-soft doll she received for her birthday this year still looks new, untouched. I *should* have seen all these things, but I didn't. Maybe I didn't want to see.

LORD, watch over my daughter who is suddenly growing up—and outgrowing her need for the dolls and toys of her childhood. Bless her with a growing faith as well as a developing mind and body.

Help me adjust myself to the loss of a little girl—and rejoice in the dawn of her womanhood. No longer will I spend hours in the toy department debating whether the blue-eyed baby or that precious fluffy-haired toddler doll would be most welcome on Christmas morning. Instead, I will debate over Honey Peach or Sparkling Pinkness at the lipstick counter, Cinnamon or Beige in the hosiery department.

So I will put a price tag on these once-cherished dolls and set them out for sale. Perhaps some other little girl's eyes will sparkle when she sees them.

But You'll understand, Lord, why I'm carefully packing just these two for storage in the attic. They're memories of a time which had to pass—an obituary for Raggedy Ann.

from MOM

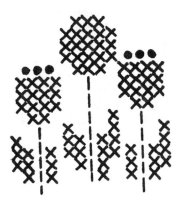

THE TEARS MUST FALL

My child was crying when she came home from school this afternoon. Between sobs, she told me that Amy was having a birthday party and she wasn't invited. "Amy said she doesn't want to be my best friend anymore. She likes Paula and Mary Alice better."

Children can be so unkind to each other. Unrestrained by social conventions and etiquette as adults are, their brutal frankness can devastate the tender young egos of playmates.

GOD, my daughter was heartbroken today. It hurts to be left out. The pain of bruised feelings can be acute. Perhaps not being invited to a birthday party doesn't seem all that important to You or to me, but it's vitally important to her.

I feel so helpless. What can I do to dry up her tears? What sympathetic words could solve her hurt feelings? I know that I can't protect my child from hurt. Growing up means learning to accept hurt as well as happiness, pain along with pleasure. The tears must fall.

But, Lord, please help her be a little stronger, a little more compassionate because of this experience. Remind her of her own hurt feelings the next time she is about to say an unkind word to another. Erase from her mind all thoughts of vengeance or "getting even." Help her to realize the golden worth of a good friend— and offer a hand of friendship to Amy at recess tomorrow. I know the tears must fall, but let them serve a worthwhile purpose in my child's life.

from MOM

28

STILL
THREE DAYS
TO PAYDAY

"I need two dollars for piano lessons." "We need lunch money this morning." "My teacher says I need $1.50 for crayons and a scissors." "Remember, it's allowance day." All I hear around the breakfast table every morning are requests for money. Little hands stretch out wide in pleas for cash.

Raising a family today is one expensive proposition. Just when I finally finished with overpriced baby foods, formulas, rattles, and rubber pants, and looked forward to an easing on the budget, they started school. Now it's lunch money, notebooks, gymsuits, and crayons!

We're not poor. My husband works hard for it but he does earn a good salary. It just doesn't stretch far enough to cover all our needs and wants. Still three days to payday—and we're broke!

Just once, *GOD*, I'd like to buy a pair of panty hose without wondering if we can afford it. I'd like to shop for a dress without looking at the price tag first and the style second. I'd like to have $5 in my billfold to buy a lipstick or magazine on impulse. Little extravagances like these mean too much to me, I know. I'm too concerned about material possessions, too vain, too selfish.

Sometimes I resent the drain my children make on our budget. Especially on days like today when I have to use the old "table knife in the piggy bank" trick to come up with a dime for Brownie dues.

Teach me, Lord, to value the priceless gift of children. They *are* expensive to raise but they're the greatest treasure in the world. If I must sacrifice for them, let me do it willingly. If I have to serve spaghetti twice this week, let me still remember to say thanks for the fresh fruit and warm bread You provided to go with it. Remind me that You'll always see us through to the next payday!

from MOM

"TEACHER WANTS TO SEE YOU"

The crumpled note clutched in a grubby hand was from his teacher. "I'd like a conference with you. Would you please come to school between 3:30 and 4:00 any afternoon this week?"

What's it going to be this time? Did he punch some little boy? Or, worse yet, a little girl? Does he need more help with his reading? Might he be held back a year? Did he give some bizarre answers on those tests the school psychologist administered to the class last month? Oh, how I dread parent-teacher conferences!

GOD, give me a cooperative and positive attitude toward this meeting. I know sometimes I think my child has no faults. I resent criticism of him even when it's constructive and needed, yes, even when it comes from someone like a teacher who has his best interests in mind. So help me go into the conference with an open mind. Don't let be be too quick to condemn— either the teacher or my child.

I thank You that my child's teacher is so concerned about him that she's willing to spend the time discussing his progress (or lack of it) with me. Apathy and indifference have no place in education and I'm so grateful that it's not present in my child's classroom. Thank You for the dedicated teachers in our school system. Won't You smile down on them and bless their classroom efforts?

from MOM

PICKING UP SOCKS AND PUTTING THEM IN THE BASKET

30

Everyone else in the family has gone off to his own pursuits. My husband to work, the children out to play with friends. All that remains behind is their mess—the mess they leave for mother to clean up!

Sometimes I get so angry I'd like to leave all the clutter and take the day off. I could coffee klatch or get my hair done or check out the dress sale downtown. Wouldn't they all be surprised to find their messes waiting for them when they got home? It would serve them right, too. They seem to forget that I'm not a paid servant. They take it for granted that I'll pick up behind them.

After all, how much more effort is required to drop a dirty sock *into* the hamper instead of *beside* it? How many seconds does it take to hang a wet bath towel on the rack or put away a set of dominoes or clear snack dishes out of the living room? And isn't it logical to assume that the person who finishes the roll of toilet paper will put a new roll on the holder? No, I guess that would be expecting too much!

I don't ask very much of anyone. Certainly I could never hope that one would actually volunteer to wipe dishes or carry out the garbage (although I often resort to coercion). I'd be satisfied if they'd just be responsible for picking up the messes they make themselves.

GOD, I'm filled with anger and self-pity again today. You know how much I dislike the thankless, never-ending duties of being a housewife. It seems like such a vicious circle with dirt and cobwebs always racing a little ahead of me. Round and round we go. I no sooner finish one task than the cleaning I did yesterday or last week needs to be redone. Keeping a clean house is, for me at least, an impossible dream (or nightmare).

But it's work that has to be done, isn't it? Won't You bless me with a happy heart and willing hands so I can face this first round of the day with a smile and a song?

I thank You for this fine home and all these possessions which clutter it. They are tokens of Your love and concern for us. Because You have provided them, I should care for these gifts with a grateful heart instead of drowning in self-pity.

I thank You, too, for my family—every messy member. A cluttered house is a small price to pay for their presence in my life. Without my husband and children, this house could never become a home. But couldn't You prick their consciences just a little the next time they make a mess?

from MOM

I'M ASHAMED OF HIM

How many ways can a child make his mother ashamed of him? Let me count them: He sits in front of the church for a Sunday school program and picks his nose all the way through the service, he wets his pants at school, the grocery store manager catches him red-handed stealing grapes from the fruit and vegetable cooler, his teacher finds the crib sheet he prepared for the exam, the list could go on and on. I've suffered through them all.

But today I knew an even greater shame than any of these. My child and his friends beat up another little boy, not because he picked on them or tattled to the teacher, but because his skin was black. I saw them waylay the boy on his way home from school. I still hear the echo of my son's voice chanting with the others, "Nigger! Nigger! Nigger!"

My child's head hangs in shame tonight, *GOD*. He knows my disappointment, my disapproval of his actions. He realizes that he did wrong; but that realization doesn't help the little black boy he hurt. No words of apology can ever completely heal the wound he created this afternoon.

Help my son to learn from this unfortunate experience. Give him empathy so he can imagine himself in another's shoes. Then give him enough love and compassion for his fellow human beings that he can offer his friendship regardless of skin color or religious faith or national origin.

from MOM

GOD ISN'T DEAD, IS HE, MOM?

I should have recognized the signs—begging off from church services, skipping Sunday school, a new type of literature finding its way to the book shelves above his desk. Among his friends the same sort of doubts, even disbelief, are emerging. But finally he verbalized his uncertainty to me. "God isn't dead, is He, Mom?"

What can I say or do to help him resolve his conflict? I can tell him of my faith but that won't help. Faith is too personal a thing to inherit secondhand from another. It must be carved out of an individual's soul by his own seeking and searching.

I can recall my own days of seeking and searching. Could my child learn from those experiences? "Yes," I told him, "there were days, many of them during my teen-age years that I questioned the existence of God. But there were also moments of insight when His spirit filled my heart so that I could clearly see the work of His hands all around me. Gradually my vision improved and my doubts evaporated. Now I don't question, I believe. But it's a belief that evolved over the years, not a gift all wrapped up and delivered in one package. It required testing and challenges to become strong and firm."

He's surprised to learn that I once stood in his shoes. But I think he's consoled by my words, too. They drive away some of the guilt that grows out of his doubts. He sees that I can accept his uncertainty and even understand it. He no longer struggles alone.

GOD, help my child in his quest for faith. Send Your spirit into his heart that he may see with new eyes. Let some who cross his path be living examples of the Christian way that he may learn from them. Give him enough patience and perseverance to continue his search even when his doubts are strong and his questions seem unanswerable.

Father, I thank You for my child's doubts and questions. Does that seem strange? Perhaps so, but I'd rather watch him fight his way through this conflict than never question Your existence at all. Strong personal faith is an active process, not a passive one. It is a living, growing part of those who believe. I pray that someday soon my child will be able to say loudly and without hesitation, "God isn't dead, Mom!"

from MOM

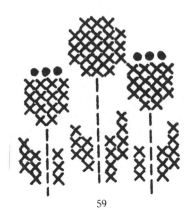

MY CUP
RUNNETH OVER

Her piece wasn't an easy selection. Certainly none of the other pupils her age attempted anything as difficult. I held my breath as she sat down at the piano, taking care to straighten the skirt of her new red pinafore and even pausing to tug the bench into just the right position. Then her fingers touched the keys in a first chord beginning a flawless rendition of the lovely and familiar melody I've heard all week at home. As I clapped (but not too vigorously), I met the eyes of other parents and smiled to acknowledge their nods of approval. It's just a piano recital, I know, but my cup runneth over.

I'm so proud of my daughter today, *GOD*. Her accomplishment wasn't just a lucky break; it was the result of hours and days and weeks of practice at the piano. There was no glory, no applause when she practiced scales and lessons—only dull repetition striving for perfection. She had her share of missed notes, skipped beats, and faulty fingering. So today's reward was earned by her own labors.

The Christian life is much like learning to play the piano, isn't it, Father? It takes years of practice and often we, too, have our missed notes and faulty fingering. I pray that my daughter will strive as vigorously, with as much determination, toward the goal of becoming a good Christian as she has toward becoming a fine pianist. Then both of us will be proud of her.

from MOM

MY PANTS ARE TOO SHORT

This morning I laid out my son's clothes and left him to dress himself while I started breakfast. A few minutes later a voice wailed from the top of the stairs, "Mom, my pants are too short!" Impossible, I thought. I bought those pants just six months ago. True, he hadn't worn them for awhile (they were crumpled in the back of a dresser drawer and had to be pressed again) but he couldn't have outgrown them already! Then he came to show me and I could see that they cleared the tops of his shoes by several inches. A wide band of blue sock which the pants should have covered was glaringly visible.

GOD, I've forgotten how fast children grow. They must stretch upward a tiny bit each day, but at times like today it seems that they've shot upward like weeds sprouting after a summer shower. Pant cuffs halt abruptly just above ankles, shirt sleeves won't quite reach wrists, the shirt bottoms can't be coaxed into covering tummies, waistbands refuse to meet and fasten, and shoes push tightly against tender toes. So soon my son outgrows his clothes.

I'm reminded again, Lord, that the years of childhood pass swiftly. Each day brings with it new growth, new knowledge, new challenges for my son to face.

I pray that You'll help his moral and spiritual growth keep pace with his physical growth. Never let him outgrow his search for Your way and Your guiding purpose in his life.

from MOM

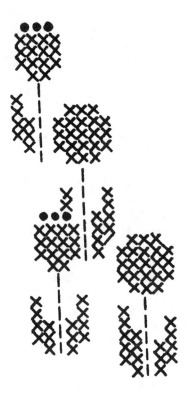

"WE NEED A SCOUT LEADER"

Another call this morning, another voice pleading, almost apologetically, "Couldn't you be scout leader this year? Last year's leader got a job and had to drop out." My spirits fell several notches. One more commitment, one more demand on my limited time. Where would I find the energy to wrestle mentally and, yes, sometimes even physically with a dozen or more active children every week?

Before long the resourceful woman had convinced me that all those helpless, malleable children would become juvenile delinquents, drug addicts, or at the very least, mildly schizophrenic if I refused the call. "Idle hands, you know," she reminded me in an ominous tone. So I said yes once more.

My husband says I'm a pushover for any good cause. I admit that I've never learned to say no. Baking cookies for PTA. Driving the scouts to their camping grounds. Chaperoning the class trip to the state capitol. Teaching Sunday school. Organizing the campaign to raise money for new playground equipment. The list goes on and on. Just when I think at last I have a breather, another call comes and I take on another responsibility—only to regret it later.

I get so tired, *GOD*, so pushed and pulled from every direction. All those books I bought and planned to read collect dust on the bookshelf. Who has time to sew or take a long bubble bath when the Brownies need a casserole for the father-daughter banquet and the Plants for the Park planning committee meets at my house tonight?

Please, Lord, help me learn to say no. Give me strength to refuse tactfully, but firmly, some of the requests which drain my strength and energy. Teach me to choose from among the many those few projects I feel are vital and worth my best efforts, commitments into which I'll put my heart as well as my hands.

Before I forget, God, thank You for my healthy body and sound mind which enable me to fulfill so many obligations. Thank You, too, for the strong, beautiful children who make all my efforts worthwhile and even, occasionally, appreciated. If I sounded un-grateful earlier, it's just that I still have to whip up a dessert for the planning committee and zip down to the store for a pint of half and half and a can of coffee.

from MOM

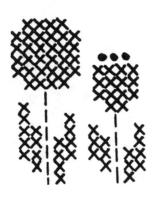

WALK
LIKE A MAN

A childhood friend of my husband's that we hadn't seen in years came to dinner tonight. When I introduced him to our son, the friend clapped him heartily on the back, exclaiming, "Just a chip off the old block, isn't he? A spittin' image of his old man twenty years back!"

I guess I can see some physical resemblance. My son does have his father's long nose, square jawline, even his big feet. He's like my husband in other ways, too. Both are soft-spoken, almost bashful. Both enjoy fishing, reading, and playing cribbage. But they have their differences as well. Many of them. My son is not a carbon copy of his father; he is a unique human being.

I recognize my son's individuality. He is separate and distinct from his father. But, at the same time, I hope that the resemblance between father and son goes much deeper than common interests and interchangeable pairs of size twelve shoes.

GOD, my husband isn't a rich or famous man. He's never won a Nobel prize or bought an oil tanker. But wealth and fame are not the blessings I'm asking for my son today.

Instead, I pray that you'll bless him with the more subtle, yet equally precious possessions of his father. Give my son gentleness and compassion. Give him a security in his manhood which doesn't rely on toughness to prove masculinity. Give him a heart capable of loving and sharing. Give him a firm faith and strong morals to help him live the Christian life. These are the traits I hope he has inherited from his father—they would be a priceless legacy.

from MOM

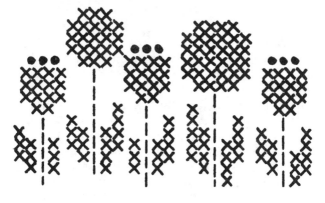

YOU BE HOME BY MIDNIGHT!

When I was beginning to date I couldn't understand my mother's anxiety whenever I went out. *Now* I understand! I'd vowed back in my younger years that I'd never stay up late at night waiting for my child to come home. Nor would I set a curfew. "I'm mature enough to know when to come in," I'd pleaded to my parents' deaf ears. Tonight my husband and I are watching the Late Show, a movie made in 1948, and listening for a car to drive up and a key to turn in the lock of the front door. And just a few hours earlier I heard him issue orders, "You be home by midnight!" It's remarkable what a few years and children of your own does to your attitudes.

GOD, have You been keeping an eye on my child tonight? I hope You weren't disappointed—that You didn't see any behavior You didn't approve of. I know the temptations my child faces with the beginning of dating are great. Body changes, new and strange desires are a part of growing up. They are natural and beautiful, but they do require maturity and control. I pray that my child and tonight's date had enough respect for themselves and each other to say no to temptation.

Is that a car coming up the street? The door clicks open and a surprised teen-ager says, "Hi, Mom, Dad. What are you two doing up so late?" My husband and I exchange a glance of understanding—and hope.

from MOM

TAKE TWO ASPIRINS AND GO TO BED

I knew when I woke up this morning that it would be a bad day. I felt sick even before I opened my eyes. For once, I didn't hurry over to look out the bedroom window, checking the weather. I just didn't care.

My body isn't well and when my body is sick, my mind and soul are troubled, too. I quarrel with my children and expect more from them than they can give. I resent the time it takes to care for their needs. They are a constant drain on my limited energy. They sap my strength, delay my recovery.

I fight back tears of self-pity or, worse yet, I give up the fighting and yield to my bottled-up emotions. The beds are unmade, dirty dishes have piled up in the sink and overflow to the counter, laundry needs to be done, and we've run out of milk! How can I cope with all this when I just want to take two aspirins and go to bed?

I need rest to heal my body, quiet and solitude to mend my troubled thoughts. But mothers have no time for rest, no opportunity for solitude. There aren't any paid sick days for us!

LORD, help me when I feel this way to remember that my illness will pass. Remind me, God, of the many, many days of good health that I enjoy and take for granted, never thinking to thank You, as I should, for each one. I often forget that life itself, whether I'm sick or well, is one of the greatest gifts You've given me. Teach me to be grateful even for this day and to use it to do Your work.

Give me the strength today to provide the love and attention my family requires. I can still manage a smile through the hurt, still listen when I'm too miserable to talk, still keep my spirit calm while my body battles off this sickness.

Make me aware of my most important responsibilities. Don't let me be too proud to ask for help. My husband would willingly pick up a gallon of milk on his way home from work if I just asked. The children might even take charge of the chores so I can rest. But first I must let them know that I need help.

Guide my faltering footsteps through this day. And when You restore my health, when my vitality and strength return, let me remember this time of sickness and learn from it. Only after experiencing bad health can a mother really appreciate being well!

from MOM

GOOD-BYE CHILDHOOD

I baked his favorite chocolate cake, iced it, trimmed it, then carried it to the dinner table, all eighteen candles glowing bright. Across the flickering flames, I saw his happy face. My eyes grew wet, then overflowed. Dumping the cake on the table, I escaped to the privacy of my bedroom. My children and my husband were bewildered by my retreat. They couldn't understand why muffled sobs drifted through the closed door.

But You understand, don't You, *GOD?* You know why this mother's heart aches. Today my son said good-bye to childhood and hello to adulthood.

I cared for him, first in my body and then all these years he's shared my life. I watched him grow from baby to lad, to teen-ager, and now to man. But on this eighteenth birthday, he's not only bidding farewell to childhood, but also to me.

Now he must stand alone as a man, forging a life for himself. He'll begin earning his own living soon, perhaps he'll marry and start a family of his own. He's not dependent on me anymore. Perhaps he hasn't been for some years but I didn't realize it until today. Somehow the years have slipped by but he'd remained my little boy, unchanged by passing time.

Now I must let go and it hurts, God. Oh, how it hurts! Worse than the labor pains which brought him into this world. More than sharing his pain and disappointments as a youth. It's a hurt only a mother can know, though probably his father also feels a twinge or two today.

Many challenges lie ahead of him these next few

years. Help him to face them with courage. His father and I hope we've given him the tools he'll need to build a happy, successful life for himself. We've tried anyway. But if we've failed somewhere or overlooked an important need, I pray that You'll make up for our negligence.

Help him, too, to face the temptations of adult life and deal with them wisely and prudently. These new rights and freedoms could overwhelm him unless Your hand steadies him through the storm. As he faces this whirling kaleidoscope of adult responsibilities, privileges, and desires, give him the strength of faith to support him.

His mother needs strength, too, God. The strength to cut the apron strings that tied his life to mine as surely as the umbilical cord once connected our bodies. Let me make the cut cleanly and swiftly, regardless of the pain it causes. Help me to accept graciously my new role—to watch and hope, to love and pray, but no longer to make his decisions or control his life.

Please bless this son, once a child but today a man.

from MOM

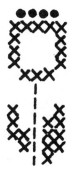

POT, VD, AND OTHER MOTHER'S WORRIES

I can't open the morning paper without reading of man's violence against man. And young people, teen-agers, sometimes play an active role in murder, rob-bery, and rape. I can't listen to the evening news with-out hearing of drug busts, drug-induced crimes, drug addict treatment. I can't flip through a magazine without finding articles on the epidemic of venereal disease, the rise of illegitimate births, the dangers of illegal abortion. These things aren't happening in some far distant place—they're occurring in my state, even my community. How can I help but worry? These are very real, very imminent threats to my child's health and happiness.

"Sure, I could get drugs without any trouble if I wanted them," my child told me recently. "They're available all over school."

Over a cup of coffee a neighbor asked, "Did you hear that the youngest Carter girl had to drop out of school? She's in a maternity home upstate."

"You wouldn't believe the number of penicillin shots I give out to young kids these days," a local doc-tor remarked at a dinner last week.

It won't help to stick my head in the sand ostrich-style and pretend that these problems don't exist. That attitude isn't only foolish, it's downright dangerous. But that's the attitude I see all around me. Parents say: "It can't be happening in my town!" or "It won't happen to *my* child." But it is, and we parents have to face the facts and attack the problems for our children's sake.

GOD, this isn't the world I would have chosen for my children. It's filled with hate, greed, and violence. But I didn't have a choice and neither will they. This is their time, their place, and they will have to live with it.

Help them to see that only the bad and ugly gets publicized but that good can still be found if they only take time to look for it. Beautiful, gentle people, unselfish actions, great and noble deeds *do* exist. They may not be spotlighted to national prominence but they can still shine as examples for young people to follow.

Help me too, Father, to worry with purpose. Passive worry just for worry's sake serves no useful purpose. But concern with action, worry which spurs a positive attack, can and has in the past changed the history of mankind. It's true that I may never be able to change the whole world but I can start with a little corner of it —right here in my own home and community.

from MOM

WE'VE COME A LONG WAY, BABY!

"What would you like to do when you finish school?" a middle-aged relative asked my daughter the other day.

She considered the question for a few moments, then answered, "I think I'd enjoy being a stock broker. Wall Street just fascinates me."

Great-aunt's eyebrows shot upward. "Don't you want to get married and have a family?"

"Oh, I guess I will eventually if the right man comes along. But I'm in no hurry to settle down."

I'm sure Great-aunt Gertie didn't expect either of my daughter's answers, nor did she approve of them. In her day capturing a husband was a young woman's first priority followed, after a proper time period, of course, by a steady succession of children. A few unfortunates like spinsters, widows, and misguided souls who didn't realize that a woman's place was in the kitchen, held full-time jobs. But they became nurses, teachers, or secretaries—not stock brokers, or telephone linemen, or nuclear physicists.

I'm grateful that my daughter's life will be different from Great-aunt Gertie's and even from mine. She will be free to choose a career and a life style which allows full development of her talents, training, and personal goals. The law and society as a whole are finally beginning to recognize the basic rights of women and the valuable contributions we can make to the world if our potential is not confined to a shuttered split-level. My daughter and her sisters can look at each other with pride and say, "We've come a long way, baby!"

GOD, I pray that she will always rejoice in her femininity. The female body is Your marvelous creation and she should be aware of it and appreciate it. Remind her, Father, that You chose a woman to nurture and bring forth from her body Your Son, Jesus Christ. A Savior born of woman. That was Your greatest tribute to women, an honor shared by all females since that great event nearly two thousand years ago.

If she should choose to marry, Lord, I pray that she'll find a husband who will value and respect her as an individual. I hope he will love her, but just as important, that he will treat her as his equal. Teach them both that in marriage their lives should run parallel with each other's as two sets of footprints across the sands of time. The tracks may be close together sometimes but they still remain separate and distinct, never completely merging.

Finally, Father, if you should bless her with daughters of her own someday, help her to teach them from her own experiences that they may become fulfilled and feminine adults, secure in their womanhood and proud of their sex. Perhaps then one day they will compare their lives with the lives of their mother and grandmother and rejoice, "We've come a long way, baby!"

from MOM

CAP
AND GOWN

I reach out to straighten the tassel on his mortarboard, then pick a piece of lint from the bulky academic gown which hangs awkwardly from my son's shoulders. "Now, Mom, you promised you wouldn't cry," this suddenly so grown up child reminds me. I nodded mutely, not wanting to reveal how close to tears I really am. Later, when I settle back into the anonymity of a darkened auditorium to watch the parade of seniors, I can release the dam. I'll be just one of many mothers weeping in happiness and, yes, in sorrow too, as we face our children's graduation.

GOD, help me to remember the true meaning of commencement—a beginning. Not an end but rather a starting line for that gigantic leap from childhood into the adult world. He will exchange school friends, teachers, familiar halls and classrooms for college or a job and, eventually, maybe marriage and a family of his own. The future holds exciting challenges and a wealth of new experiences for him. I pray that You'll give him strength to meet his new life boldly and with courage.

Both my child and I face new beginnings tonight. I, too, am a graduate leaving behind the care of a baby, a child, an adolescent—my familiar role as mother. Help me to find a new purpose in life to fill this void left by my graduating senior. Show me the route my own commencement should take. Guide this graduate and his mother in the directions You want us to go.

from MOM

WITH THIS RING . . .

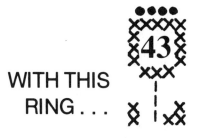

An organist playing the wedding march, tall white candles burning brightly, baskets of flowers flanking the altar—the perfect setting for a wedding. At the altar stands a young man dressed in an uncomfortable and unfamiliar tuxedo. Approaching him now, on her father's arm, the bride he's chosen to build a life with. She's radiant, with that freshness only youth can know and happiness shining through her nervousness. Here, in the front pew, I watch all the pageantry with a personal eye. My child will soon be married.

Tears well up and overflow. I'd promised myself I wouldn't cry but the emotional impact of the occasion is too great. Once a baby that I cared for, now an adult ready to assume the responsibilities of marriage and perhaps eventually a family. The years are compressed, condensed into one brief moment. One minute I am giving birth, the next I give away a child. But I do it freely, willingly, hoping that marriage will bring to my child the same unique joy it has to my husband and me.

GOD, Bless this partnership joined before your altar today. They have pledged their love and exchanged rings as a token of a commitment to each other that only death can break. But You know, Father, that too many wedding vows are broken, too many marriages end in a divorce court. Surely that must sadden You and make You disappointed with the man and woman You created. I pray that You'll help this young couple weather the storms of marriage and come out into the sunshine and rainbows with an even stronger devotion for each other.

Keep them true to each other despite the temptations to stray. One man, one woman for a lifetime. But if one should err, give the other the strength to forgive and enough compassion to forget.

If You should bless their union with a child, guide them as parents. Let their love be reflected in the fruit of their togetherness.

All these things I pray today—on my child's wedding day.

from MOM

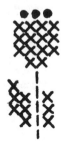

LET ME
CALL YOU
GRANDMA

An excited stammer transmitted across the telephone wires to my kitchen: "Good morning, Grandma. It's a boy!" The proud father assured me that both mother and baby were doing fine. "And I think he's got Grandpa's nose." My heart swelled up with emotion too great to convey in words. I am a *GRANDMOTHER!*

LORD, it seems like only yesterday that my husband shared the same exciting news with two other sets of eager grandparents. The cycle of life is now complete —birth, giving birth, and finally, a new life which will eventually replace mine. A chain of generations stretching back to Creation now adds another link. I thank You that my grandson is healthy and his mother survived the labor and birth.

These new parents will need your guidance, Father. They are both young and inexperienced. A baby is Your great gift to a marriage but still it alters two life styles dramatically. Help this mother to love and care for her child, but never to forget that she is a wife as well. Give the father compassion and understanding of his wife's new role so that he'll assume greater responsibilities and willingly share the task of raising their child. Remind them both that a healthy marriage, like a plant, needs nourishment to grow and that the finest gift they can give their child is parents who live together happily and lovingly.

Teach me to be a good grandmother. When I might meddle or interfere where I have no right, hold me back. When I want to offer advice, still my tongue until I am asked. When I am about to criticize, whisper a warning word in my ear. The responsibility for this infant grandson belongs to his parents. They should be free to raise him as they see fit without outside pressure from my generation. Remind them that they can always turn to You for answers.

Over the past two decades I've asked many blessings for my child. I've come to You countless times with his problems and mine, and You've always shown us a solution. I've prayed to You in my child's name that he might become strong in mind, body, and more important, his Christian faith. Now I ask, not as a mother but as a grandmother, that You'll shower these same blessings upon my new grandson.

from GRANDMA

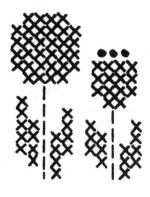